Stubborn Faith

Rodney Martin

authorHOUSE®

AuthorHouse™
1663 Liberty Drive
Bloomington, IN 47403
www.authorhouse.com
Phone: 1 (800) 839-8640

© 2016 Rodney Martin. All rights reserved.

No part of this book may be reproduced, stored in a retrieval system, or transmitted by any means without the written permission of the author.

Published by AuthorHouse 10/13/2016

ISBN: 978-1-5049-3226-4 (sc)
ISBN: 978-1-5049-3252-3 (e)

Library of Congress Control Number: 2015913367

Print information available on the last page.

Any people depicted in stock imagery provided by Thinkstock are models, and such images are being used for illustrative purposes only. Certain stock imagery © Thinkstock.

This book is printed on acid-free paper.

Because of the dynamic nature of the Internet, any web addresses or links contained in this book may have changed since publication and may no longer be valid. The views expressed in this work are solely those of the author and do not necessarily reflect the views of the publisher, and the publisher hereby disclaims any responsibility for them.

KJV
Scripture quotations marked KJV are from the Holy Bible, King James Version (Authorized Version). First published in 1611. Quoted from the KJV Classic Reference Bible, Copyright © 1983 by The Zondervan Corporation.

Contents

Introduction ix

Part 1

How to Use Your Gifts to Change Things

Chapter 1: Your Relationship with God 3
Chapter 2: Be True to Yourself 11
Chapter 3: Help Somebody 17
Chapter 4: Be Passionate About Your Goals 23

Part 2

Faith, Family, Friends, and Fun

Chapter 5: Enjoy Your Life and Laugh a Lot 31
Chapter 6: Love Your Kids 35
Chapter 7: Always Put God First in Everything 41

Part 3

Positive Thinking Is a Ticket to Success

Chapter 8: Operating Your Own Business................47
Chapter 9: Volunteering to Make a Difference in the World 51
Chapter 10: Going the Extra Mile.............................57
Chapter 11: Three Secret Prayers Each Day................61

Part 4

Mustard Seed Faith

Chapter 12: Storms Will Come 67

This book is dedicated in loving memory of my grandmother Bertha Martin and my aunts, Blondell Jenkins and Evelyn White. Even today I carry memories of all the lessons and kindness you showed me with your sweet love and concern for my life and future. Because of this kind of love that I received, I am somebody. Love you, Mom. Thanks, Dad. Thank you guys for producing me.

To my wife, Lamonica Martin. Thank you for believing in me and helping me with this project. I love you.

To my children, Kinslee, Tiyanna, Ramel, Lester, and Sylvester. I love you with all my heart. What a blessing it has been to raise all five of you. As life goes on, never stop dreaming. Always put God first in all that you do and you will have lots of success.

To all people of all races, creeds, nationalities, origins, this is a message from God that I pray will strengthen your well-being and allow you to reach out to others who need to be empowered as well.

I also want to thank those who have been praying for me. I send a special thanks to all of my siblings, who have witnessed my growth from a young boy to a successful entrepreneur. Thank you for all of your love, support, and patience with me throughout the years.

A special thanks to my sweet mother-in-law, Gladys Lee, who has been an important icon in my life since I met her.

Finally, I want to thank you for purchasing my first book. I pray that it will give you the vision, guidance, and motivation to succeed in life. I also want to encourage you to do all you can to make a positive difference in this world, seek to inspire those who need to be uplifted, and always be mindful of the less fortunate.

Introduction

This is the beginning of my first book, which will show that I belong in the business of writing. I pray that God will continue to bless me and allow me to reach people through my positive motivation and inspiration. In today's world, there a lot of people need to be lifted up and encouraged. I find that people in general tend to blame others for their lack of motivation, especially if life has been hard for them, so I'm convinced that you have to be your own booster. When things get tough for you, that's when you must have faith, believe in yourself and your dream, and never give up on yourself. Life will be very difficult at times, but you can overcome any situation in your life by being a true believer in the word of God. When the pressures of life seem to be getting you down, that's the time to hold on to your inner faith, which will enable you to keep pressing on, toward your life goals.

Part 1

How to Use Your Gifts to Change Things

Chapter 1

Your Relationship with God

Hello, and how are you? I am writing this book with permission from God, hoping and praying that it will help get your life on the right track. I once was lost, but now I'm found; I was blind, but now I see. I did not always have a serious relationship with God, but through the prayers of the righteous and my desire to make changes in my life, I was able to make a conscious decision to trust and serve God. The very first thing you must do is fall to your knees and ask God to forgive you for your sins. No matter what you've done or are still doing, God will forgive you. You see, God is not like humanity; he loves us unconditionally.

A relationship with God is a lifetime commitment to trusting and serving him no matter who or what comes your way. This is not an overnight success but a strong, dedicated, and positive attitude to stay on the right course. Once you make up your mind to serve God, you must be willing to suffer the pains of life without losing your faith. As the apostle Luke said to theLord in Luke 17:5–6, "Increase our faith." So the Lord said, "If you have faith as a mustard seed, you can say to this mulberry tree, 'Be pulled up by the roots,' and it would obey you."

This is such a small amount of faith that God is speaking of, but you will only develop this kind of faith through a serious relationship with him. No matter how rich or poor you are, just remember that you must have your mind made up to serve the Lord in order to enjoy the fruits of the spirit, because the mind is truly a terrible thing to waste.

You have to be bold in your walk with God because fear will have you doubting your faith in him. When you set your mind and heart to accomplish something in life, never give up on those dreams; just keep pressing your way through. All of a sudden, you will find yourself at the top of your mission. In life, you are either in it or out of it, but you can't allow your fears to cause you to give up on yourself. Life is brief. You can't afford to not trust your own ideas, because no matter who we are, it will be over soon. Developing a sincere and passionate relationship with God must be an urgent part of your life while blood is still running warm through your veins.

As you yield your life to him, I challenge you to live for him so that you can become a witness. Once you yield your life to Christ, your problems and difficulties won't necessarily vanish, but now you will have the power to fight off enemies without using guns and knives. Instead, you will be able to use the teachings of the Bible to help others become better people. Being saved by the grace of the almighty God is not some kind of fashion show where you put a piece of clothing on and then take it off once the show's over. This is a way of life that you must live because souls can be saved through your living and giving.

A good relationship with God will allow you to exceed the expectations that others have put on your life. Knowing that you have a powerful backup system that you can call on at any time, day or night, especially when life deals you an awful hand, gives you that extra confidence. The future will be full of blessings when you have true confidence that things will be okay, because it will allow you to focus more on your success.

Once you become successful in life, you will definitely need a strong connection with God because he will help you stay grounded and thankful for his many blessings. But why wait until you make it before you start serving God? Always put him in front of you, and don't just take him casually, because he is the alpha and the omega of all things known to man.

A sincere relationship with God will help you deal with all kinds of traumatic situations. A lot of times this will create peace, love, and happiness when there is doubt or trouble. I strongly feel that when you acknowledge God as head of your life, you make him smile down from heaven and he rewards you accordingly. But you must always be thinking about him in everything you do. This mind-set will allow you to keep on striving and reaching for the stars.

The moment you think it was you who acted is the time when things will gradually slip away from you, because God is a jealous God who demands that we acknowledge him in all things through his son, Christ Jesus. It's okay to give yourself the benefit of the doubt sometimes, but to God be the glory at all times, especially when he brings you out of a tough situation that no one else has the power to. Each of us has such a unique way of connecting with our spiritual center, and even though the methods may be very different, the goal is the same.

Developing a foundation of confidence in yourself is essential to really connecting with God. It will help you when God is trying to tell you something but you are listening to others with no power who cannot tell you anything that will help you. Take the leadership role in your life and fulfill the divine assignment you were given.

Trust your own ideas with outrageous sacrifice because you know more about what will complete your task in life, especially when it's something phenomenal. Be the most confident booster in your life because nobody knows you better than you, and do it with desire and gratitude because that's what God expects from you.

One of the greatest motivational moments in my life was in the 1980s when I was listening to the late coach Jim Valvano as he gave one of his last speeches. He said, "No matter what you are going through, just never give up. Never give up." Mind you now, this man was dying of cancer, but he had such a positive attitude in fighting for his life that I knew he had to have been in communication with God and had God on his side to speak so vibrantly.

When you become sick and tired of being sick and tired, it's time to board this train, which will enhance your future and give you a peace of mind that only God can give. I challenge you to think about your life so you can make a conscious decision to call on the name of Jesus for his love and forgiveness because he is all you need. In this life, you are either in it or out of it; which do you choose?

When you have the tools of the spirit positioned in your life correctly, you can achieve immeasurable heights because this will give you the added motivation you need in order to become successful. I encourage you to read books by people who have made it and are willing to share their stories. How can you apply some of their knowledge toward your life goals? Follow that voice in your head that says to you, *Yes, you can.* The reason it's so hard to stay focused on the positive things in life is the negative press that surrounds us all, but you have to be a very keen thinker for yourself and not allow the critics to cause you to quit, because if you do, you will have given up on yourself and your loved ones.

In my opinion, the number-one reason people fail in life is their weak connection to the vine. Without a strong connection to Jesus Christ, it is impossible to please God because he gave us all the information we need on our journey. It is such a powerful thing to be well connected to God because now you have a power station that will never lose an ounce of energy. So build your house on a solid foundation with God. He has promised us that he will give us the desires of our hearts.

Stop trusting people who never show you examples of Christ through their living. Just because they have material wealth doesn't mean they are good for you, so be wise in making decisions about who your friends are. Be friendly toward all people, but don't give your heart to everyone who seeks it unless he or she has demonstrated a true and trustworthy relationship with you. When you have built a strong foundation with Christ as the head of your life, you begin to see things from a totally different vantage point; it empowers your dreams and ideas. When you have a dream that you can do or become, don't quit until you have exhausted all your plans, and even after that, you have to dig deep into your heart and mind to find the extra willpower. Spiritual maturity is crucial in your walk with God. You must grow in your faith as you experience great challenges that people or situations present to you; that's the purpose of accepting Christ, so you will be able to resist the temptations and frustrations of the world and not lose control of your mind.

Once you mature in your Christian walk, you will be able to help those who may not be there yet. I suggest that you make a serious sacrifice to grow by reading and studying God's word and attending church every Sunday. Also go to Sunday school, where you can have daily discussions about how to walk closer with God.

The level of maturity I'm speaking of is, for example, when you do some work for someone as a self-employed business owner and that person refuses to pay you. What do you do? This has happened to me on many occasions in my painting business, and here is how I handled it: I immediately went to God in silence with a prayer of forgiveness for the client who betrayed me, but I did let him or her know that God knows and sees all that we do. Each time I handled it in that way, I grew even closer to God as a matured Christian.

You must remember that vengeance belongs to God, and had I handled the situation improperly with physical violence, I would be locked away in a prison cell somewhere away from my family, the ones I was trying to work for and support. One of my special mentors who helped enhance my career, the late Dr. Maya Angelou, wrote, "Do the best you can until you know better. Then when you know better, do better." I use that quote all of the time in my business and everyday life because it is one of the most simple and self-explanatory pieces of wisdom you can absorb.

Chapter 2

Be True to Yourself

When you tell that family member or friend or stranger that you love him or her, mean it from the heart because if you don't mean it, you are not being true to yourself or the other person. Try to use self-loyalty toward each and every thing you do in your life and learn to be happy about it because God loves a cheerful giver.

Your character is a makeup of attitude, loyalty, trust, and charisma, and if you exercise those characteristics, you have no choice but to be an outstanding and caring person. Also when you are true to yourself, you live longer because stress and poor attitude leads to many sicknesses and diseases that can probably be avoided if you just take more time out to care about yourself. For example, when was the last time you had a serious workout at the gym or the basketball court?

Be aware of your health at all times. Go to the doctor if you feel unwell. Try to take better care of this great temple that you were blessed with because we owe that to ourselves. Start somewhere. No matter what condition you may find yourself in, you can come out of it with just a little faith and confidence. So stop all of the negative thinking and be a believer in something for the first time. With this kind of positive attitude, you can bring about so many good things in your life,

It was some thirty-two years ago when I got saved and was converted to serve God. Before that I was in a terrible state of mind. I didn't want to believe I needed help, and I ran from place to place, doing all the wrong things like drugs, alcohol, crime, and sex just to feel macho. I can recall the very moment that I took time out for myself to attend a church revival one summer night back in 1984. I heard a voice from God saying, "Come to me," and when the preacher asked if anyone wanted to be saved, I said yes to myself and had the courage to go up to the front of the church to ask for prayer. That prayer changed my life forever.

I recall the late Dr. Reverend Virginia Tucker, who took me under her wing and visited with me for hours after church one Sunday until I was calling on the name of Jesus and the demons poured out of my soul. Oh what an experience that has been to remember because of the life that has followed me since that day. I can tell you that I have been on this journey for a long time, but that's not to say that things have always been good because I'm a Christian. I still have my challenges in life, but because I have accepted Christ as my Lord and savior, I now have joy, peace, and love, which enables me to handle the crises that I face in a more spiritual manner verses wanting to get even with people who betray me.

When you put on the whole armor of God, you now have power to fight against the devil and his crew, who will always be in attack mode, trying to get you to turn back to thinking and acting negatively. I thank God for allowing me the opportunity to share some of my gifts with you in hope of getting you prepared for a breakthrough in your life, but you must do like I did some thirty-two years ago: make up your mind that you want to change and have enough guts to admit that to God, and I promise that your life will never be the same.

If this is true in your life, make a few changes and watch your stock start to rise. Stop blaming others for your failures in life; that's the easy way out. Just remember that you are in total control of your own destiny. If you fail, don't quit. Just brush yourself off and try it again. I believe that every person has the ability to be something great if he or she seeks first the kingdom of God. Then, as he promised, everything else will be added unto your life. If you are afraid to challenge yourself in your efforts to become successful, you will miss out on a true blessing. Failure is not an option when you are focused on your dreams and goals. You have to be very stubborn in all that you do and never give up on yourself.

When you set out to do something great, always remember that your honesty toward your goals will allow you to stay on course and never quit. That's why it is so important to develop an "I-can, I-will" type of attitude, which will give you victory over any situation. Trust your inner self with a tremendous amount of faith. You don't want to procrastinate on things in your life that can end up being a blessing for you and your family.

You have to spoil yourself with God's love in order for you to love yourself unconditionally because in this life we need to be self-confident in all that we do in order for us to be pleasing in the sight of God. Being honest and caring toward others gives you pure energy to do more in your life, along with a healthier mind and body.

The truth will set you free, especially when it comes to yourself. Don't try to be something you are not because you will be living a false life, and that's not something that pleases God. So get your house in order and go after your dreams with a tremendous amount of force. A good name in this world is worth more than silver and gold, so protect it. Just be yourself.

When you have an idea to take action or be great, keep it locked inside until you have evaluated your progress and determination. This will give you a clear sense of direction that you need to follow. It will also enable you to trust your own ideas more. Too many times we put ourselves and our dreams on the backburner. This type of action causes us to fail. Be more loyal to yourself. You are your biggest supporter in this world.

For example, you want to be a movie star because everybody tells you that you look like you should be in Hollywood, but deep down inside your heart you hate acting. Don't try to be something your heart is not in agreement with, because you won't put forth the effort to make it come true. When you hear that voice in your head telling you to do something and it's the right thing to do, don't wait on someone to give you the okay. Just preserve your thoughts and move forward with a smile. If you are not faithful to your own life, there's no way on God's green earth that you can be faithful toward others. So I challenge you to treat yourself with pride and dignity and not be a fake.

I can take you back to my early years as a young man who was searching for happiness. I was introduced to alcohol and drugs at the age of fifteen, and I began to hang out with the wrong crowd. I was drinking wine, beer and liquor, but I tried to hide it from my grandmother, who was a Christian woman, so I had to really keep my focus on respecting her home. The habits I developed caused me to lose focus on my dreams and aspirations in life. I also allowed the peer pressure to influence me to try new drugs and other forms of getting high. I started to smoke cigarettes and marijuana.

By the age of sixteen, I was a junkie using all kinds of pills and drugs. I can recall several mornings getting ready for school and feeling like I needed to have a drink before I could leave the house. I would have some of the older guys who were seniors buy wine for me, a wine called Mad Dog 20/20. I was in serious trouble at this point in my life, but in spite of all the drugs and alcohol, I was able to take the gift that God had blessed me with and perfect my skills as a basketball player. Even though I was not quite healed from my mess, I still was able to focus on my future of becoming a professional basketball player.

Several years passed, and I continued to battle my many addictions. I believed that I could overcome the demons that seemed to have me. By the ripe old age of twenty-one, I really wanted to change for good, so I considered going to college. I enrolled in 1981 and wanted to play basketball. I asked people who the coach of the basketball team was, and I literally stalked him outside the gym to ask him when tryouts were going to be held. He gave me the date and told me to come prepared to try out for the Morris College team.

I say all of this to emphasize that when you have a dream that is fertilized with purpose and passion, you can make it a reality, as I did. I not only made the college basketball team, but I also made the starting five, which was unheard of prior to my coming to play at Morris College. I also did this again in 1985 at another college called Columbia Junior College. I was invited to try out for the basketball team there. I attended training camp and found myself competing for the starting position as a shooting guard. I eventually won that position as a starter on the team. In doing so, I proved to those who said I couldn't do it that hard work and dedication paid off.

The most important thing I can say to anyone who believes in him- or herself is never give up on yourself and pursue your dreams with all of your heart and mind.

Chapter 3

Help Somebody

The ability to help someone is one of my favorite gifts that God has blessed me with. When I help someone I get a high that no drug can give me. One of the ways you will know if you have the gift of giving and helping is if when you do it your heart feels good and you never complain about helping or giving, even if you're helping a total stranger. The Bible, 2 Corinthians 9:7 tells us to let each person give as he or she purposes in his or her heart, not grudgingly or out of necessity, for God loves a cheerful giver.

I have some good advice on blessings. When your day has gone badly and everything that can happen has happened and everything that you could try has failed, just go out and visit a hospital or say a few kind words to someone. From that experience alone you will gain so much appreciation for your circumstances and problems that you will shout, "Thank you, Lord!" If all the people in the world did this for just one day, imagine the kind of world this would create for the people who have no one to show them love. Before you complain about something, remember that some can't speak a word because they are in a coma at the local hospital, and when you want to help somebody and a friend or family member is saying not to, just remember that whatever you are trying to give is pleasing to God.

When you help people, your kindness can produce positive motivation that can perhaps save their lives. It will also have God smiling down upon your life from heaven with wonderful blessings. One of my favorite sports slogans is from a company called Nike: just do it. They kept it real and simple, and that's all God is saying to us. This kind of action will guarantee the favor of God because his word is true and powerful. Heaven and Earth may pass away, but the word of God will last forever. What else do we need, people?

In this life, if you can help somebody to accomplish his or her dreams, do it, because you will be judged by God according to your good works on this earth, not how much money you had or how famous you were. I would even say that the more you share of your thoughts and ideas, the better your life will be because God will give you a whole new set of plans and dreams. So always be willing to help someone who is reaching out for advice and motivation. Your skills and knowledge were not given to you for just self-satisfaction.

There are times in this world when we all will be tested in our faith, but that's not the time to throw in the towel. It is the tests and trials that will help us grow. So

I challenge you to be strong in your struggles and to go out into the highways and byways and help others who may not be as strong as you. By sharing those powerful testimonies that God has given you, you can perhaps save someone's life or help someone get it right. If you become a true soldier for Christ, I guarantee you that everything you ask of God, he will do. (However, do understand that while he may not come when you want him, he is always on time.)

The word *help* means to aid or assist. When you develop an attitude that wants to help out, in critical times or in good times, it gives you peace in your heart and mind because as you think about the person or situation that your kindness affected, you begin to smile on the inside and the outside, and this alone, in my opinion, can improve your heart's function. So, my brothers and sisters, go out there and help make this world a better place for people who need us. If you are trying to help make a difference in the lives of people, just remember to be genuine with them and have a committed heart to their pain. They will notice if you are sincere.

When you help someone, don't ever look for a return favor from him or her. Just know in your heart that you just pleased God because that's what he wants us to do and because one day you will need help. And who knows? That same person may have to help you. It doesn't matter if you are rich or poor, white or black, because God made us all in his own image, and there's nothing we can do to change that, so we might as well accept our differences and move forward. There are so many ways that you can make a positive difference in this world by showing love toward all mankind and stopping stereotypical attitudes.

When this life is over, we will be judged by God himself, and it won't be on how famous we were or how rich we were but instead what did we do for his people. Consider what the Bible says about a rich man entering into the kingdom of heaven: "For it is easier for a camel to go through the eye of a needle than for a rich man to enter the kingdom of God" (Luke 18:25). Be careful where you put your trust because if it's not in God, you will lose in the end when you die. Learn to trust in God enough to share your wealth with the less fortunate.

For example, if you are financially stable, go out into the highways and byways and seek to make a difference in others' lives. I'm not saying give them money. Donate your time to talk to them. Maybe you can discover who needs financial help or just some good old encouraging conversations. That's what pleases God. He's not impressed with your wealth or money. Remember, he is the one who blessed you with everything that you have. When you are rich, you must be very careful how you treat those who are poor. God can make the same poor person you once mistreated your boss by downsizing your assets and increasing that person's financial portfolio.

I'm not saying that having money is a bad thing, but I believe that the Bible is saying that if you do have money, don't think it guarantees you a place in heaven. While you live on this planet, you ought to be about helping others to reach their dreams in life because someone helped you.

I want to share with you the stories of several people who took it upon themselves to help me when I was a young lad. The late Mr. Moses Drakeford was like a big brother to me. He always believed in me. Coach Drakeford said I had the talent as a football, baseball, and basketball player to become something in life and have a good future. He assured my grandmother that he would take good care of me. He came by my house and picked me and my brother up for practice and then brought us back home safe. He told me that if I could stay out of trouble and do my school work that I had a good chance of making it in sports. He was a high school teacher who knew the importance of a quality education. I was very fortunate to have a positive mentor in my life just when I needed one.

The second person is the late Dr. Daisy Belton Alexander. She was so encouraging and enthusiastic about my life because she knew my grandmother and they were friends. She is responsible for some of the successes that I'm enjoying today because she would always tell me that if I wanted to be something in life, I could become it. She was my math teacher in seventh grade, and boy what a teacher she was, one who helped build her students' self-esteem to a level where they could see themselves getting better and better. Later on in life, some ten years later, our paths crossed again. I had finished high school, and she was a college instructor at Morris College. Once again she asked me if I wanted to attend college. I said yes, and to this day I don't remember how I was able to enroll in college, but she helped me with all my paperwork and I was accepted to Morris College. She was a pioneer in our community of Camden, South Carolina

These are just a few important people outside of my family who really made a difference in my life, and I thank God for allowing me to meet them. I would ask that you acknowledge the people were there to support you in your life when no one else would. Those are the people who were sent from God to see about you. When you become that successful businessman or businesswoman, don't turn your back on the less fortunate. Develop a habit of reaching out to help in a positive manner. Become a mentor to young boys and girls.

I also encourage you to read some good books about others who have become successful in life, and I'm not just talking about money. There are so many forms of success that can open doors for you in life. I recall reading a book by Dr. Ben Carson in which he said that knowledge and hard work are more important than houses, cars, and bank accounts. I agree with him because in order to acquire all of the finer things in life, you have to have the knowledge and work ethic to achieve greatness.

In your life, do not be afraid to dream big. Small dreamers receive small awards, and when it's all said and done, you will get what you ask for in faith. When you began to share your testimonies to others, be strong in your delivery. Let them know that you trust in a higher power. For each and every thing that you get, don't just be satisfied with getting your foot in the door. Work hard to make your spirit and ideas heard.

Chapter 4

Be Passionate About Your Goals

When you decide to pursue your goals and dreams, you must develop a sincere love and dedication for it, meaning that no matter what happens, you will continue to work toward it. Passion is another gift that only God can give you when you humble yourself in his word. When you are passionate about something, it doesn't matter what others say or think of your idea unless they are giving you important and useful information that you can use to help you along the way.

Also, don't be afraid to set your goals high. If you put God first, ahead of your life goals, then and only then will they become possible. In my opinion, one of the major reasons people fail is fear, Fear will destroy your motivation for success because it limits your creativity, which will cause you to quit on yourself. In order to conquer your fears, you must know whose you are and what you believe in. You must also have a blueprint in your heart and mind on how you plan to accomplish your goals. Never give up on yourself, even if others give up on you. This includes your family members because sometimes they will not understand how important your success is to you. You have to be your biggest booster.

Here's a true example of how passionate I was in the eleventh grade. One of my teachers asked me what I wanted to be when I got older, and I said a professional basketball player for the Philadelphia 76ers of the NBA. A lot of my classmates laughed at me, but little did they know, I was very serious. Upon graduating from high school in 1980, I started training and dedicating myself to basketball. In the fall of 1981, I enrolled at Morris College in Sumter, South Carolina, where I tried out for the basketball team as a walk-on and found myself not only competing for a spot on the team but a chance to be the starting wing guard as a shooter.

When the final roster was assembled, my name was on there. I had made the final cut and was also recognized as one of the best athletes on campus. After playing for one season at Morris, during the summer of 1982, I began to work at a textile mill in Camden, South Carolina. While riding with a coworker on a delivery, I hurt my neck and back when we got into a wreck. But I was determined to get back into shape, and I started rehab, which took several months.

When I was ready to play again, I joined the recreation league. I felt good about my progress, so I decided to give college another shot. This time, in 1985, I enrolled at Columbia Junior College in Columbia, South Carolina, where I walked on and made the team once again as a college basketball player. This time was different because I had become sober and accepted Jesus Christ. That is what gave me the victory that I needed to be the best. I was a starter, but I knew I had to work hard because I was the best player at my position. I shot the ball well and played tremendous defense against opposing teams. But this was the best experience I could have had at that time because it taught me how to be a better team player.

After graduating from Columbia Junior College in 1987 with an associate's degree in business administration, I worked several jobs, but the passion in me was still burning to play professional basketball. And believe me, it was pure passion and determination that elevated me to the next level as a professional athlete.

In 1989, the Charlotte Hornets became the new NBA expansion team, and they contacted me by phone with an invitation to attend their rookie free agents basketball camp, which was held in Charlotte, North Carolina, at the YMCA. After my arrival for the camp, I stayed with a friend for two weeks but was contacted by my family to let me know that my grandmother wasn't doing well. I made up my mind to go back home to be with her and help take care of her.

Once I arrived back home in Camden, South Carolina, I received a letter from the Charlotte Hornets director of player personnel, Mr. Bill Shelton, that said the camp had been cancelled because of a lack of quality participants and if things changed, I would be contacted. Enclosed with that letter was the first and only paycheck I would receive from the Charlotte Hornets. It was a thrill to see the NBA symbol of Jerry West on that check, and it motivated me all the more. I knew that if you could dream something in life, you could surely do it if you stuck to it and never gave up on yourself. The moral of my story is not that I made lots of money or even played basketball in the NBA, but that you can be all you want to be if you learn some very important characteristics of your life and passion.

None of those things would have happened if I hadn't developed a serious and personal relationship with God. I believed that I was good enough and qualified to play professional basketball in the NBA. Even though I never got the chance to play in the league, I value my strong commitment to God for blessing me with courage and faith. The reason that so many people give up and quit in their lives is their lack of passion, faith, and motivation. They want things to happen quickly, but patience is a virtue, especially if you want to become successful in life. If you develop the kind of attitude that says to God, I will trust you no matter what happens or who tries to get in the way, He will make a way out of a dead end and build a foundation on a spiritual life, not a material one.

God has promised to give you the desires of your heart, but you have to put in the work. When you seek success in life, you must surround yourself with positive people who have dreams and ideas because you can feed off one another. I encourage you to write down your goals, plans, and ideas because sometimes you can forget or become distracted. I recall reading a Inspirational book by Chris Gardner, titled The Pursuit of Happyness where he talked about life lessons in getting from where you are to where you want to be. He said to start with what you have in your hand.

There will be times when everything that can go wrong does, but that's when you have to be determined and keep pressing forward toward your goals. You must develop an "I can, I will, and I must" attitude to eliminate the possibility of failure. Success is controlled by your state of mind.

When you apply passion toward your goals and dreams, you will have much success. Passion will lead you as you prepare for the task at hand, but that's not to say it will be easy. It will simply make sense to keep working toward your goals according to your vision because you will have discovered your inner strengths. Passion is simply love of doing something that you have always believed you could do.

So once you decide what you want to do, attack it with great passion and commitment. In doing so, you will find more reasons to keep going instead of giving up.

Part 2

Faith, Family, Friends, and Fun

Chapter 5

Enjoy Your Life and Laugh a Lot

There is a time in all of our lives when we must put off all the excuses for why we can't be happy and joyful. A sense of humor will go a long way in your life because it will allow you to balance the everyday stresses. Believe me, I know it's hard to laugh when your rent is due and you don't have the money, but that's when your relationship with God is supposed to enhance your positive mind-set.

In order for you to really enjoy your life, you must love and accept who you are as a human being. Self-love and self-motivation will allow you to be happy when others think you should be sad and lonely, and help you stop blaming others for the sad and unfortunate situations in your life. We all will face challenging times, but we must not allow them to separate us from our faith in God.

Have some fun, but make sure it's clean fun that will not send you to prison or destroy your health. If you have to use drugs and alcohol to have fun, that's not real fun. There are so many things that sound like fun, but once you get involved they become disastrous. So use good judgment and wisdom to help you live a good, clean, and positive life. Find something that you enjoy doing and be very passionate about it because it will bring peace and happiness to your life for many years to come.

So hold your head up and smile because God has a plan for your life. But first, in order for you to reach your full potential, you must put on the whole armor of God.

When you laugh, you make your internal organs feel refreshed. This will help you to think better and control the high levels of stress that you deal with daily. The reason so many people are suffering from anxiety and depression is because they internalize failure as a permanent option instead of a temporary setback that they can overcome. In this life, you will face some challenging days, but if you don't internalize them, they will pass you by like a mighty rushing wind on the ocean shore.

Humor can be very good for your health because it allows your mind to just relax and forget about your troubles. When you laugh about your experiences or someone else's experiences, it helps you move on to the next phase without an attitude. So go out to a comedy show just for a good ole laugh or watch some funny television shows. Get away from the news and the violence because it will drain all the positive energy out of you. Though you should always keep up with the current events happening in society, you should also know how to escape from it without feeling that you will miss out on something important.

Keep your eyes on the prize and stay tuned in to your dreams. You have all the creative ways to make your dreams happen, so stop making all kinds of excuses for not getting them done. When you fail a test, you have to find some sort of humor to allow you to rethink your life's possibilities and to stop killing your positive thoughts with negative doubts.

Rise above all things that are not showing you favor, including people. Be self-supportive with the wisdom you have developed from your past mistakes and challenges. You will begin to smile and laugh once you discover who you really are.

Find time to share with others who also need to laugh. Call up a friend and tell him or her a joke without telling a sob story. Your healing will come when you learn how to enjoy where you're at, knowing beyond a shadow of a doubt that God is going to bring you out. I can recall watching the movie *The Pursuit of Happyness*, starring Will Smith, and it inspired me so much because his character always had a humorous side even though he was going through so much at home and at his job. It is an inspiring story of how this incredibly determined man made it to the big-time boardroom.

In your pursuit you have to be happy knowing that you will arrive soon. So I encourage you to start where you are and don't worry about how you will finish. Just know deep down in your heart and soul that one day you will prevail. I know it's sometimes hard to make yourself happy and cheerful, but when you make an internal evaluation of your life, there is always something inside you that will give you the clue to keep going.

Chapter 6

Love Your Kids

When I say love your kids, I'm not just talking about telling them you love them. I'm talking about setting good examples for them through the way you live so that they can have a road map that they can trust and follow for the rest of their lives. You are the most important person in your children's lives because they look to you for guidance, leadership, and other life skills. For example, if you don't want your kids to smoke or drink, then don't do it around them. This is not to say that they will never do it, but if they eventually develop those habits, they won't be able to blame you for their failures. Good parents are always very careful about what they say and do around their children.

If your kids don't live with you, frequently call them on the phone or e-mail them a positive message. Talk to them about drugs, crime, and sex because if you don't, the streets will educate them with the wrong information. When you care enough to have those important discussions with your kids, they will one day respect all that you tried to tell them, even if they end up making a few mistakes in life.

The Bible speaks about how we must raise our kids: "Train up a child in the way he should go: and when he is old, he will not depart from it" (Prov. 22:6 KJV). God will hold us all accountable for the rearing of our children, so please don't take it for granted that it's not our jobs, because it is our responsibility. The most important thing to remember, parents, is that in order for us to be effective leaders as parents, we must be parents who live by the word of God in all that we do and say. We must educate our children on the principles of God because this will give them a good foundation upon which to build the rest of their lives, especially as they become parents one day.

When I was a young boy, my grandmother raised me on those same principles of God, and I will be the first to say that I went astray from her teachings. But as I matured as a man who was taught correctly, I began to understand it better. That's what I would call growing pains. If you are a positive parent to your kids even when they make mistakes in life, you can have a good impact on their futures because they will recognize that you are real.

Now, this doesn't mean that you drop your guard and allow them to escape their discipline. Discipline will show them that you are dedicated to the cause. It took a village to raise me because in my younger days if I did something wrong, my grandmother knew about it before I got home. That's because of the neighborhood watch and all the people who cared and wanted me to become someone who did not get into trouble. In today's world, society has developed a system that encourages kids to call 911 if their parents put their hands on them, but I disagree with that system because all it does is make children more disrespectful toward their parents.

When your child does something wrong, don't be so quick to say you know he or she would not do that. Peer pressure will affect every child at some point in his or her young life. That's when children will make a mistake and do something they were not supposed to do. You have to be the kind of parent who will not become your child's best friend but instead preach and teach love and support and set good examples.

In order for you to be an effective parent to your children, you have to show them tough love sometimes because they will stray off course and head in the wrong direction. At the same time, you should never talk down to your children. Even if they've done wrong, you have to be a forgiving parent who will forgive them and pray for them. But do voice your opinion to them in an authentic way, which will show them that you still love them in spite of their troubles. All they really want to know is that you still care.

Be supportive of your kids by attending their school activities on a regular basis. This will give them more self-confidence when they are with their peers because kids do talk among themselves about their parents. You want to be a good parent. If your children participate in sports, teach them that winning is not everything and that having fun and doing their very best is what competing is all about. Then, if and when they do make it as a professional athlete, they will have the wisdom to know how they must conduct themselves.

Teach your kids how to say the Lord's Prayer and make sure they always bless their food before they eat it because one day they might meet another little kid who doesn't know or was never taught these things and they could be such a blessing to him or her. Be fair with your kids but don't take them for granted. They want to know that you love them unconditionally, so develop a pattern of supporting them in all of their activities. If you are the kind of parent who wants your kids to become successful in life, just remember to set some good examples through your faith. Always be courteous and respectful, and show and teach them how to live.

Parents, stop emphasizing the wrong things when it comes to your kids. Don't worry about their swag and whether they are dressed in the top name-brand clothes and shoes. Instead, teach them about the powers of prayer and God. Tell them to put a high value on their manners, and teach them how to respect other people. Also stress the importance of a quality education. These are some of the things that can prevent your kids from ending up as statistics in our growing prison population. Also understand that a lot of it is not the kids' fault. Our society also contributes to the unjustified ways in which some kids are viewed.

I strongly believe that if we as parents begin to fish for the souls of our kids rather than the surface, that's what will make kids value their lives more. It seems to me that today's youth don't value their lives and the great opportunities they have as much as past generations did. In past generations, we didn't have the great technology that we can use today, such as the Internet and cell phones. While some kids use this technology for advancement in life, a lot use it for all the wrong reasons. As a parent, I think you should have control of what your kids watch on TV and how they surf the Internet because the bad guys are waiting for them. I know it's not possible to know everything your kids do, but if you prepare them well, the future results will be rewarding.

I also challenge all men to teach your girls how to be respectful young ladies. You can do this by respecting their mothers and taking them on dad-daughter dates to show them how a boyfriend should respect and love them. If you have sons, it is critical to teach them first and foremost to respect all women, even if the women don't want them to be gentlemen. This includes opening doors for women, pumping the gas in their cars, washing their cars, helping them with homework, and talking *to* them, not at them. I also think that as a parent you must set good patterns of love and peace in your home for the kids to recognize that it's something they want one day.

Chapter 7

Always Put God First in Everything

Seek ye first the kingdom of God and you will have so much fun and success in all your life's endeavors because God is a jealous god who demands that we consult him first.

When you are faced with challenging moments in your life, just remember that Jesus died on the cross so that you could have the right to the tree of life. Forgive those who hate you or say all sorts of evil things against you. This is probably one of the hardest things to do as a human being, forgiving someone who has violated your trust, but the Bible says do not be overcome by evil, but overcome evil with good (Rom. 12:21).

I will admit that this is hard to do, but it is possible, and all because of God's grace and its sufficiency, especially when you come to know and trust God as the Lord and savior of your life. God knows that we are weak and need his love and strength. That's why he sent his one and only begotten son down to earth to die on the cross for our sins and said that whosoever believes in him shall have life everlasting. Once you have consulted with God about your situation, then there is a time to be patient and wait on his answer and instructions before you make your next move. If you try to do anything in life without first talking to God about it, my sisters and brothers, it will not work. It will seem to for a while, and then all of a sudden the bottom will drop out because you were disobedient to God's word.

The word of God is and should be your map to achieving your goals and dreams in life because with God all things are possible. I encourage you to develop a plan for your life, write it down, and start working toward it so that you can accomplish it. I truly believe that every human being has a plan, but a lot of us use all kinds of excuses as to why we can't do it. Only when you face your fears head-on will things begin to change for you. It is okay to fail, but it's never okay to quit, because once you quit, you have given up on your dreams in life. If you lack faith and confidence in yourself, you have failed at least 99 percent of life's test because your ability to go the extra mile on your journey toward success all depends on your attitude.

If your health is failing you and you need healing, just trust God. If you can't pay your bills, just trust God. If you are experiencing hard times in other areas of your life, just learn to trust God. You can do nothing without him but everything with him. That's why it's important to get closer to him. Try repenting your sins as God has requested in his holy word. If you want to be a true blessing to someone, just try Jesus for yourself. Then you can be a testament of how good he really is. God will forgive us our sins, but we must be connected to him through our faith and love. That's how we can gain favor from God when things beyond our control happen.

Part 3

Positive Thinking Is a Ticket to Success

Chapter 8

Operating Your Own Business

This is a part of life that everyone dreams of one day, and if you pray, plan, and prepare, this can be for you as well. When you decide that you want to operate a business, be very serious about it. Create a good business plan as to how you will make it happen. You must be prepared to deal with the uncertainties of being a business owner. To be an effective and successful business owner you must have a true and committed relationship with God. Remember that your customers are always right, even if you know they are wrong, because this will show that you have what it takes to be successful. Don't be afraid to voice your opinion to the customer, but make sure it is in a positive tone of voice.

In your own business you must market yourself as a trustworthy person through your actions and not just your words because this is the epitome of what you do. You also must have a broad vision of how to attract good business people to your organization so that you can increase your sales and grow your business as expected.

I have some good advice for people who want to make a lot of money as business owners: never go into a business just for the money because you will get burned out quickly and as soon as sales decrease you will quit. So I advise you to do your homework. Plan, research, and prepare for the journey you are about to take. Talk to others who have similar businesses, see how they did it, and from that develop a strong strategic plan and don't look back.

I also say that if you start a business, make sure it is legal because if it isn't, it will suffer from a lack of quality leadership. Yes, it may bring in lots of money for a while, but eventually it will fall flat on its foundation and may cause you to lose your freedom or your life. So be wise and do the right thing.

When you decide to open a business, the first thing you need to do is your homework. Set some plans and follow them accordingly. Read some good books on business and go to workshops. Learn first of all what your business's purpose is and be very positive in your approach. I also encourage you to write down all the things you want to add to your business as you grow it, Have some short-term goals and some long-term goals, and even if things don't go as planned, just remember that you are successful because you took the first step in your future dreams and plans when you decided to start a new business.

I also suggest that you talk to people who have done great things in business. Don't be afraid to ask successful people questions. I do it all the time. This kind of attitude will help you create an explosive business that's full of potential. I will warn you that operating any business is a serious challenge because it's totally up to you to set it up for a lifetime of success, but when you have self-confidence and a committed spirit, you will be equipped to fight for the longevity of your business.

Be very professional in what you do for others. The number-one thing to focus on is the customer. I will never tell you to set your rules based on the concept that the customer is always right (because in reality the customer is not always right). Instead, set your rules so that when the customer is wrong you will be able to explain how you can fix the problem to suit their taste. In any situation you face with a dissatisfied customer, try to offer a quick resolution to the problem. That won't always work, so you have to rely on your spiritual attitude and try to be respectful, even if respect is not being displayed toward you. That's what God's love will allow you to do for a disgruntled customer.

You must also be willing to help those who come to you for simple advice and not use one of the old slogans like "I got mine the hard way, so you got to get yours." Remember, God loves a cheerful giver, and it's not always the giving of money that pleases God. Sometimes it's just caring enough about a person. I also advise that when you create your business plan, you should develop a habit of volunteering your time to some agency or place where you can possibly get a contract. It's called networking.

In business you have to invest countless hours and days trying to create new vehicles that will take you to the places you need to be.

One of most important factors for creating success is persistence. If you hear a lot of no's, keep going until you hear a yes. A yes will indicate that you've arrived, but it doesn't necessarily mean that you have conquered anything special. You have to be open to accepting critiques and abuse from your peers and sometimes your competitors, but don't you dare let them stop you.

Also remember that if you first dreamed of becoming a business owner, it was not by accident. So get in the groove and make it happen for you and your family. Do a lot of research and get all the information on your business together. But most of all, make sure you have the passion to match the dream of business ownership.

Chapter 9

Volunteering to Make a Difference in the World

$\mathcal{W}$hen things in your life just don't seem to be working in your favor, you must still keep a positive attitude about your life and your life's work. Begin to fall down on your knees and ask God to show you the way because someone else is hurting worse than you are. I suggest that you start helping others who are less fortunate than you. In doing this, you will discover that your problems are nothing that you can't overcome.

The good thing about giving and volunteering your time to help others is that you will draw closer to God and he will bless you abundantly. "So let each one give as he purposes in his heart, not grudgingly or of necessity; for God loves a cheerful giver" (2 Cor. 9:7). Paul is saying that once you develop a passionate attitude toward others and give your time or money to help make a difference in someone else's life, you will be rewarded by God himself with favorable blessings.

It is very important to care about others by demonstrating the gifts that God has blessed you with to help others fulfill their pursuit of happiness. Just tell a total stranger that you love them and that God will make a way out of no way. When you activate the love that's inside your heart and share it with someone else, it is such a beautiful thing and it will add years to your life. Find something that is bigger than you and work toward making it successful for others to enjoy. You can't be selfish and negative if you plan to become a true motivator.

The word *volunteer* can change your life in many ways because it can introduce you to people and things that will have an everlasting effect on your life and your future. When you dedicate time to bring a smile to another person's face, this is such a joy to experience and it empowers your mission toward your goals in life. But when you give of your time, it must come from your heart. You know in advance that you're not getting paid to do it. That's why you have to have a strong spiritual attitude in order to help others without any regretful taste in your mouth.

The one thing you don't want is to help someone and then hate that you did it. You would be letting God down if you did that. So make sure you aim to help when you do give your time or resources. I started a nonprofit foundation in 1984 through my hometown church, Mt. Zion Baptist of Kirkwood, and my mission was to help educate young people on the dangers of drugs and alcohol because of what I had been through. I wanted to share with them some of the real-life experiences that made me take a long hard look in the mirror one day.

Today, some thirty-two years later, I'm still on the battlefield, volunteering my time and energy, trying to make a difference in someone's life. When you do it with great passion you will help make this world a better place for others, so I encourage you to find something that you can do for others who may not be able to do it for themselves.

When you volunteer your time to whatever cause, do it with love and compassion. It will make a difference in the lives of people who just need to see that you care for them. You never know; your smile or your kind act may be the only one they have experienced. So be a good, faithful witness for Christ.

I enjoy helping young people through my foundation, Athletes Against Drugs, because it gives me hope and inspiration for my own life. I have many dreams and visions of success for young people, and God has blessed me with the gifts and passion to make a difference in the world. I can recall when, in 2010, I helped with a youth basketball camp in Georgia. After the camp was over, the kids were hugging my legs. What an awesome feeling that was. Those kids were inspired by the way I treated them at the camp.

If your life is not going the way you want it to go, try volunteering a small amount of your time. Go visit a hospital, nursing home, or prison and you will discover that your life is worth living because there are people who would love to be in your place. So try to develop an attitude that will allow you to reach out to those who need to hear kind words of support and comfort.

This world is full of people who volunteer their time to others, but deep down on the inside those people don't want to do it. This is not showing true Christlike love. If you are doing it for money, then you are not authentic in your relationship with God. So whatever you decide to do, make sure you are being led by the spirit of God. When you volunteer for the right reasons, the money and support will come because God will send the right people and resources into your path of life for you to be successful for the kingdom.

I think every for-profit business should have a nonprofit attitude toward people, meaning they should value every human being and be willing to help. When you give some quality time to aid in the success of someone else, it empowers your dreams and makes your business more profitable. I take deep pride in volunteering my time to teach kids the fundamentals of basketball because it brings me joy and happiness, which enables me to continue on my journey of success and teachings.

I'm currently a basketball coach and life coach at my daughter's school. One day I was out sick and the response I received with all the positive things that those kids said to me through the giving of cards was so overwhelming and touching that I thought I needed to share some of them with you.Message number one.Thank you Coach for teaching us Basketball skills,you have made us proud of ourselves.number two.Dear Coach Martin,you have taught me how to shoot a Basketball.You are awesome,you can even have your own shoes called The Martins.number three.Thank you for preparing me for life lessons,you are a great coach I want you to be my Basketball coach when I grow up.

Chapter 10

Going the Extra Mile

*I*n this life you must be willing to go the extra mile to get things done. Sometimes it all depends on how badly you want it. If you want great results in your business or personal life, then you have to be totally committed to putting in the time. If you don't put in the time, then you should not complain when you are not prospering.

You will be challenged by the difficulties and unfortunate circumstances that will sometimes follow you throughout life, but you must not let them control your mind. Instead keep trying to create better ways to attack the situations. If you are an athlete who is trying to make it to the NBA or the NFL, I have some good advice for you: Train harder than anyone else by disciplining yourself according to a work ethic that sets you apart from all others. Those extra hours in the gym or on the court will give you an edge on the competition. And, yes, it will show in all that you do because you will be hungrier than most. In life, don't look for the easy way out. Always be willing to work harder. When you do this, your expectations will likely be met.

I was fortunate to have positive people in my life who always supported me and went the extra mile to make sure I had a roof over my head and food and clothing. This is why I continue to reach out to those who are less fortunate, so that I can help them build their courage muscles. In going the extra mile, you will encounter turbulence and problems, but you have to have a made up mind that nothing or no one will stop you. Believe in all the things that God has given you to fight with, and when you are tired, just get a good night's rest and get back at it the next day. Don't allow anyone to stop you from moving on.

Is life hard sometimes? Yes, it is, but that's all the more reason to keep going because if you don't quit, you will make it there, just where you belong at the top. Be stubborn in all that you do, without any doubts or fears. This is the kind of attitude you must have when you are a big dreamer in life.

One of the pupils I mentor named Julian texted me and said, "Mr. Martin, do you think I can make it to the NBA?" I responded, "Yes, you can, but it's going to take a lot of training, running, and endurance to be in the best shape of your life." I also shared some other attributes that he must have, such as a healthy lifestyle of no smoking, drinking, or drugs and involvement with a church, which would give him structure and discipline.

He said to me after I told him how old I was (at that time I was fifty-two) that he also wanted to know I how jumped so high, so I explained to him that my dedication to health has allowed me, with the blessings from God, to be able to still soar with the best of them. He was very eager to know how to get his body in shape for basketball. I told him that I still trained hard and ran, lifted, and shot hoops every day and that this helped me not only to stay in shape but to still believe that I could play basketball in the NBA with today's great youth.

If you set your goals in life high, even if you don't reach them, you will fall somewhere in the universe on top of something good. Just remember that when you have a dream, it's not your idea; it is a blessing from God, who gave it to you. In order for you to reach your dream, you have to follow what's in your heart and what's on your mind and never allow anyone to persuade you in the wrong direction.

To be the best, you have to act and think like you're the best because all your power comes from your own thoughts. Now that's not to say that you can't draw strength and wisdom from someone else, but the true foundation to all your success comes from you. If you are running in a race and you have not trained properly, do you expect to win? It's the exact same principal in real life, so I hope and pray that you develop some dynamic tactics that will give you a chance in life. If you are not motivated by your own dreams, how can you motivate anyone else who seeks knowledge from you?

I think every living human being has several dreams in life, but the biggest thing that hinders them is fear. They are afraid and it's easy to find all kinds of excuses instead of doing the extra things it takes to make it. As a result, they come up with all of the many reasons why they can't do it. The world is full of procrastinators who say things that sound like a good idea, but all the while they are in pain thinking about it.

I want to make a recommendation to all of you who are seeking greatness and dreams: surround yourself with individuals who talk and walk like you. It is a contagious disease that you want to catch, because this kind of disease will bring healing to your soul. On this journey you will discover that you are stronger than you thought you were. You may have to shed many tears at times, but just know that in the end each tear will be dried from your eyes by your own smile, and it's going to be a bright smile that no one will be able to wipe off your face.

So, my brothers and sisters, continue to strive for greatness with all your might through your faith in God, and one day you will find yourself accomplishing more than you expected. Be authentic toward all that you do and appreciate every trial and tribulation that you encounter along your journey because if you don't have any, you're heading in the wrong direction.

What are you thinking about when you dream? Do you really want it? Can you see yourself in a vision of that dream? If you can answer these questions for yourself, then keep working hard to make it happen for your life and your family.

Chapter 11

Three Secret Prayers Each Day

When you talk to God in privacy, it is the best time to really say what you want to say without any limits. He wants you to express all your emotions to him and give him all the glory, honor, and praise. You should pray in secret so that you can put all of the negative ideas to rest, knowing that your prayers will be heard and answered. But you must understand that if you don't have a sincere personal relationship with God, your prayers will seem impossible.

In my opinion, most people give up praying too quickly because they don't have one of the most important ingredients of the spirit: patience. Just because you go to church every Sunday doesn't mean that your relationship with God is tight. When you pray to God, you have to wait on his answers. It may not happen when you want it to, but it will always be on time.

When you set aside that moment to pray to God, it lets him know that you are thankful and sincere, so don't fool yourself by thinking that God doesn't know your heart. Just try to work on yourself until you get to that level of passion for serving God.

Being at work should not stop you from praying. You can be both in a business meeting and secretly praying to God at the same time. So don't ever give the excuse that you have no time or place. The three prayers a day, one each for the father, son, and Holy Ghost, is the pathway to all of your success in life, so take it very seriously. However, if you only pray once a day, that's still okay. Just pray.

Be courageous when you pray. Don't worry about who is watching you, because everyone must give an account for him- or herself. Prayer has always been the key to success, and your faith will always open the doors you are trying to get through. So do yourself a big favor and develop a prayer life, one that will create opportunities beyond measure. Why try to do it on your own? Proverbs 3:5–6 says, "Trust in the Lord with all thine heart; and lean not unto thine own understanding. In all thy ways acknowledge him, and he shall direct thy paths" (KJV).

I am a witness that a prayer life makes a big difference in a person's life. You now have a power source that will enable you to move mountains out of your way without having to lift a finger. You will just use that supernatural gift from God to guide you in the right direction. You will experience nothing in life from which prayer can't deliver you. Absolutely nothing.

Also remember that when you say a prayer, you need to have faith enough to believe it will happen. Even if it doesn't happen when you want it, know that it's always on time when you need it. Be confident when you call upon God to do something for you or your family. Why ask for something when you know you have doubt about the outcome? God answers all our prayers, but the answers may not always be in our favor. That's when your faith has to be at work, and you must be able to accept his answer without anger or frustration.

Sometimes God delays us just to test the faith that we claim to have in him. I would say that if you haven't gotten the answers you're looking for, keep the rivers of joy active in your heart and mind. When your prayers are answered, go out into the world and be an advocate for Christ. Be willing to share the good news with others who you know need to hear it. This is not a selfish kind of thing that you need to hold on to; it's an unselfish act that you ought to be proud to tell to others.

Did you know that it was God who gave you that mind to want changes in your life? I would ask that you place unlimited value on that very thought and nurture it with love. Prayer changed the way this world has been formed, with great leaders, mentors, businessmen, and businesswomen. Some of our forefathers may not have admitted that it was prayer that brought about changes in our society, but I believe that prayer is why I can sit here at my computer and write a book. My grandmother always told me that she was praying for me.

I challenge you in your efforts to reach success, try prayer and then let me know how it worked for your life. Because when you trust in God and not man, you have done what he requires of you.

Part 4

Mustard Seed Faith

And the Lord said, If ye had faith as a grain of mustard seed, ye might say unto this sycamine tree, Be thou plucked up by the root, and be thou planted in the sea; and it should obey you.

—Luke 17:6, King James Version

Chapter 12

Storms Will Come

When you decide to go after your dreams in life, obstacles can get in your way, but you must know how to exercise your faith in God. That's why you must have a strong mind and a serious commitment to believe in yourself.

Just when things seem to be going right, all of a sudden everything that can happen will happen. That's when you have to be still in the midst of the storm instead of throwing in the towel and quitting. You must always be aware of people, places, and things that don't mean you well because they will destroy your focus along your journey to success. But do pay close attention to things, and if you fail the first time, don't internalize your failure. Instead, get up and try it again.

In life you are either in it or out of it. You must decide which one fits you because I guarantee you that if you don't take a stand for something, you will fall for anything. Be of good courage and faith and don't blame the storms of life for your failures. Instead use them to enhance your character as a positive person who believes in God. Once you see yourself as a successful person in life, don't allow anyone to make you feel that you are not. Negative people can cause you to lose focus on your dreams. They will drain all of your positive energy, and once they do that, you will start to feel helpless and hopeless.

If you don't fail from time to time, then don't look for success. Failure is good for your psyche. It teaches you how to better prepare yourself and your ideas. It makes you go back to the drawing board for more knowledge. I also encourage you to read books about successful people who have failed but didn't allow their failures to cause them to quit. For example, one of my favorite mentors is Tyler Perry. If he had given up after being turned down several times, his main character Madea wouldn't exist and all of his successes would be void. But he stayed true to himself and believed in his ideas.

I don't want to discourage you, but when you set your sights on becoming rich and successful, don't think it's going to be pain free because you feel that you deserve your dreams. It doesn't work that way. You will experience lots of pain and disappointment on your journey through life, but just remember the passion you have for it.

When you are challenged by difficult tasks in life, just remember that they are part of your success. You must go through many dangerous snares and difficulties in order to make it, so learn to accept the bad. It's only temporary. A blessing is on the way if you prepare yourself in the correct manner. The good thing about all of this is that once you go through it, you will have knowledge and strength, which will prepare you for even greater challenges in the future.

When you have faith in the supernatural gifts that only God can provide, you become more expecting of goodness rather than searching for it in some other person or thing. That faith becomes your powerful source of being and belief in your dreams and values. Always speak highly of yourself when times are rough because this gives you a positive source of energy to contain all matter of evil that's being directed toward you. Be very encouraging during your storms in life. In order to do this, you must have very serious talk with God just to confirm that your relationship with him is valid and real.

A storm can come in many forms, but the question is how you deal with each one. My experience of how to deal with a storm is that you must recognize the storm and its ingredients in order to resolve it effectively. When a storm shows up, most of the time it catches us off guard. We often try to ignore them, but we must have the courage to attack storms head-on. If you could see each and every storm that comes your way, the road would be easy. Unfortunately, that's not always the case. That's why you must put on the whole armor of God so that the storm will become transparent in your life.

Storms will not stop coming for as long as you live, but if you are connected to the vine, the storms will cease. In today's society, some of the most dangerous storms are media based. This means that someone has targeted you with false accusations or is just trying to tear you down. That's when you have to be able to draw strength from your faith.

I say to you today that when you are faced with difficulty and are trying to survive the hardships of life, remember that you have the ability to change your situation by renewing your thoughts and actions. When you are struggling to pay your bills, just keep believing in God for change and do not destroy your own spirit with unfaithful doubts. Instead encourage yourself by saying, "I can do all things through Christ, who strengthens me." Believe it and receive it from the Lord.

When you are facing a terrible storm, first of all you must believe it won't last forever and that this too shall pass. If you can stay positive long enough to seek the right kind of instructions from God, most of your worries will end. If you try to handle your storms without first seeking God, then you've lost before you even started because you are lacking the power to create change in your situation or circumstances. Get some power from the right source of energy, which can only be found in Christ Jesus. You can defeat any storm in your life if you have the correct attitude and are willing to fight with faith and love.

You don't need anyone's approval. Approve yourself.

—Les Brown

Made in the USA
Lexington, KY
18 March 2017